Ms. Sally's

Healthy Habit

CALENDAR JOURNAL

Ms. Sally's

Healthy Habit

CALENDAR JOURNAL

For Kids

SALLY BRADLEY

A Ms. Sally Book-www.Leemitt.com

Printed in the United States of America

Publishing services by Selah Publishing Group, LLC, Tennessee. The views expressed or implied in this work do not necessarily reflect those of Selah Publishing Group.

ISBN: 978-1-58930-251-8
Library of Congress Control Number: 2010903104

"Motivation is what gets you started.
Habit is what keeps you going."

— Anonymous

JANUARY

The Positive Word Seed: Attitude

at·ti·tude
Pronunciation: \ˈa-tə-ˌtüd, -ˌtyüd\
Function: *noun*
Etymology: French, from Italian *attitudine,* literally, aptitude, from Late Latin *aptitudin-, aptitudo* fitness
Date: 1668

1 : the arrangement of the parts of a body or figure : posture
2 : a position assumed for a specific purpose <a threatening attitude>
3 : a ballet position similar to the arabesque in which the raised leg is bent at the knee
4 a : a mental position with regard to a fact or state <a helpful attitude>
b : a feeling or emotion toward a fact or state
5 : the position of an aircraft or spacecraft determined by the relationship between its axes and a reference datum (as the horizon or a particular star)
6 : an organismic state of readiness to respond in a characteristic way to a stimulus (as an object, concept, or situation)
7 a : a negative or hostile state of mind
b : a cool, cocky, defiant, or arrogant manner

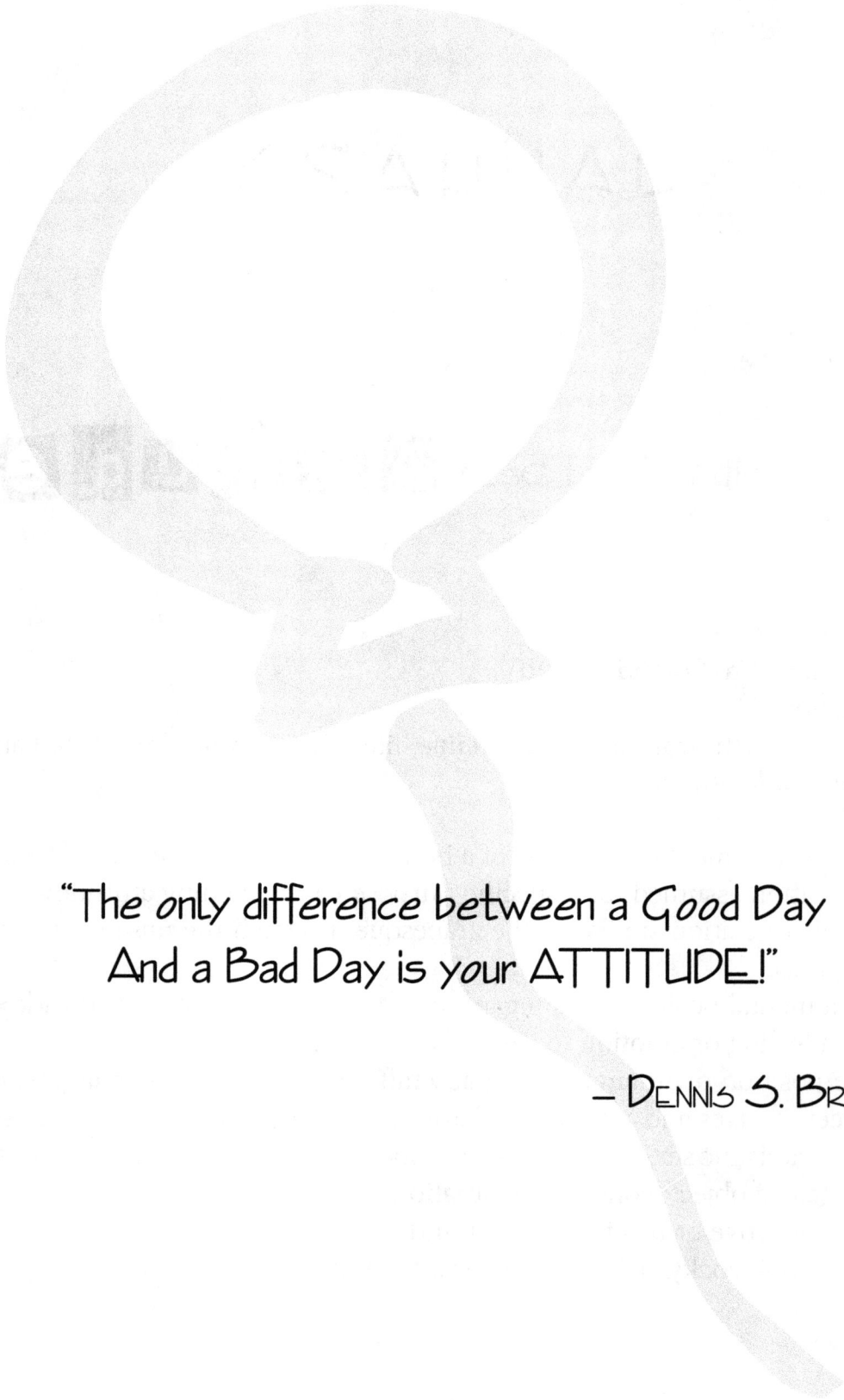

"The only difference between a Good Day
And a Bad Day is your ATTITUDE!"

– Dennis S. Brown

Action Steps

☐ Sunday ______

☐ Monday ______

☐ Tuesday ______

☐ Wednesday ______

☐ Thursday ______

☐ Friday ______

☐ Saturday ______

January

Attitude

Week 2

Positive Reinforcement

☐ Sunday ____

____

____

☐ Monday ____

____

____

☐ Tuesday ____

____

____

☐ Wednesday ____

____

____

☐ Thursday ____

____

____

☐ Friday ____

____

____

☐ Saturday ____

____

____

Role Playing

☐ Sunday

☐ Monday

☐ Tuesday

☐ Wednesday

☐ Thursday

☐ Friday

☐ Saturday

January

Attitude

week 4

Growing

☐ Sunday

☐ Monday

☐ Tuesday

☐ Wednesday

☐ Thursday

☐ Friday

☐ Saturday

Notes

January Notes cont.

FEBRUARY

The Positive Word Seed: Behavior

be·hav·ior
Pronunciation: \bi-'hā-vyər, bē-\
Function: *noun*
Etymology: alteration of Middle English *behavour*, from *behaver*.
Date: 15th century

1 a : the manner of conducting oneself
b : anything that an organism does involving action and response to stimulation
c : the response of an individual, group, or species to its environment
2 : the way in which someone behaves; *also* : an instance of such behavior
3 : the way in which something functions or operates
— be·hav·ior·al \-vyə-rəl\ *adjective*
— be·hav·ior·al·ly \-rə-lē\ *adverb*

"There's never a wrong time to do what's right."

- Unknown

Action Steps

- [ ] Sunday ______________________________

- [ ] Monday ______________________________

- [ ] Tuesday ______________________________

- [ ] Wednesday ______________________________

- [ ] Thursday ______________________________

- [ ] Friday ______________________________

- [ ] Saturday ______________________________

February

Behavior week 2

Positive Reinforcement

☐ Sunday ______________________________

____

____

☐ Monday ______________________________

____

____

☐ Tuesday ______________________________

____

____

☐ Wednesday ______________________________

____

____

☐ Thursday ______________________________

____

____

☐ Friday ______________________________

____

____

☐ Saturday ______________________________

____

____

Role Playing

☐ Sunday ______________________________

____

____

☐ Monday ______________________________

____

____

☐ Tuesday ______________________________

____

____

☐ Wednesday ______________________________

____

____

☐ Thursday ______________________________

____

____

☐ Friday ______________________________

____

____

☐ Saturday ______________________________

____

____

February Behavior Week 4

Growing

☐ Sunday ____________________________________

____

____

☐ Monday ____________________________________

____

____

☐ Tuesday ____________________________________

____

____

☐ Wednesday __________________________________

____

____

☐ Thursday ___________________________________

____

____

☐ Friday _____________________________________

____

____

☐ Saturday ___________________________________

____

____

Notes

February Notes cont.

MARCH

The Positive Word Seed: Nutrition

nu·tri·tion
Pronunciation: \nu̇-'tri-shən, nyu̇-\
Function: *noun*
Etymology: Middle English *nutricioun*, from Late Latin *nutrition-, nutritio*, from Latin *nutrire*
Date: 15th century

1 : the act or process of nourishing or being nourished; *specifically* : the sum of the processes by which an animal or plant takes in and utilizes food substances

2 : nourishment 1

— nu·tri·tion·al \-'trish-nəl, -'tri-shə-nəl\ *adjective*

— nu·tri·tion·al·ly *adverb*

"Don't be the one you see
but the one you want to be."

-Unknown

Action Steps

☐ Sunday ____________________

____

____

☐ Monday ____________________

____

____

☐ Tuesday ____________________

____

____

☐ Wednesday ____________________

____

____

☐ Thursday ____________________

____

____

☐ Friday ____________________

____

____

☐ Saturday ____________________

____

____

Positive Reinforcement

☐ Sunday ______________________________

____

____

☐ Monday ______________________________

____

____

☐ Tuesday ______________________________

____

____

☐ Wednesday ______________________________

____

____

☐ Thursday ______________________________

____

____

☐ Friday ______________________________

____

____

☐ Saturday ______________________________

____

____

Role Playing

☐ Sunday ____________________

☐ Monday ____________________

☐ Tuesday ____________________

☐ Wednesday ____________________

☐ Thursday ____________________

☐ Friday ____________________

☐ Saturday ____________________

Growing

☐ Sunday

☐ Monday

☐ Tuesday

☐ Wednesday

☐ Thursday

☐ Friday

☐ Saturday

Notes

March Notes cont.

APRIL

The Positive Word Seed:

communication

com·mu·ni·ca·tion
Pronunciation: \kə-ˌmyü-nə-ˈkā-shən\
Function: *noun*
Date: 14th century

1 : an act or instance of transmitting
2 a : information communicated
b : a verbal or written message
3 a : a process by which information is exchanged between individuals through a common system of symbols, signs, or behavior <the function of pheromones in insect communication>; *also* : exchange of information
b : personal rapport <a lack of communication between old and young persons>
4 *plural*
a : a system (as of telephones) for communicating
b : a system of routes for moving troops, supplies, and vehicles
c : personnel engaged in communicating
5 *plural but sing or plural in constr*
a : a technique for expressing ideas effectively (as in speech)
b : the technology of the transmission of information (as by print or telecommunication)
— com·mu·ni·ca·tion·al \-shnəl, -shə-nəl\ *adjective*

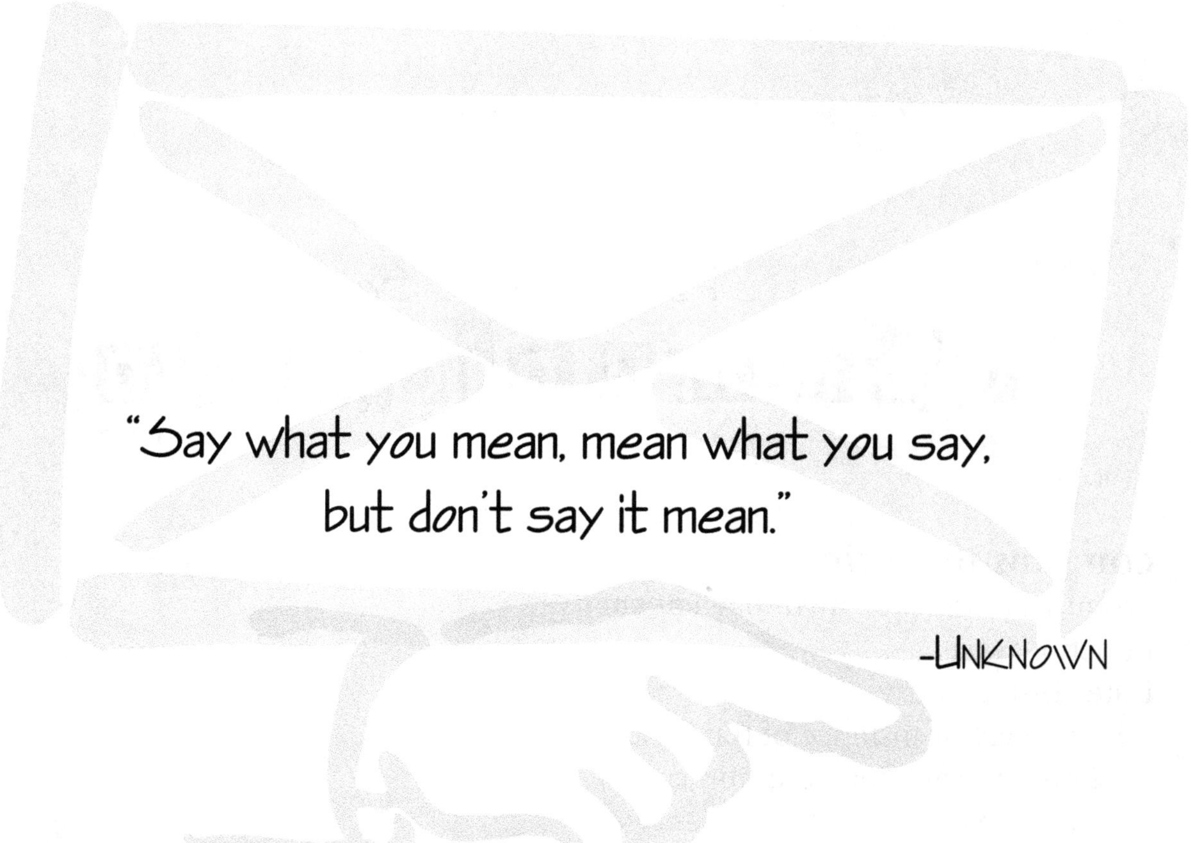

"Say what you mean, mean what you say,
but don't say it mean."

-Unknown

Action Steps

☐ Sunday ______________________________

____

____

☐ Monday ______________________________

____

____

☐ Tuesday ______________________________

____

____

☐ Wednesday ______________________________

____

____

☐ Thursday ______________________________

____

____

☐ Friday ______________________________

____

____

☐ Saturday ______________________________

____

____

Positive Reinforcement

☐ Sunday ______________________________

☐ Monday ______________________________

☐ Tuesday ______________________________

☐ Wednesday ______________________________

☐ Thursday ______________________________

☐ Friday ______________________________

☐ Saturday ______________________________

Role Playing

☐ Sunday

☐ Monday

☐ Tuesday

☐ Wednesday

☐ Thursday

☐ Friday

☐ Saturday

Growing

☐ Sunday

☐ Monday

☐ Tuesday

☐ Wednesday

☐ Thursday

☐ Friday

☐ Saturday

Notes

April Notes cont.

MAY

The Positive Word Seed:

Table-Manners

Table Manners: A pattern of behavior that is conventionally required of someone while eating.

man·ner

Pronunciation: \'ma-nər\

Function: *noun*

Etymology: Middle English *manere*, from Anglo-French, from Vulgar Latin **manuaria*, from Latin, feminine of *manuarius* of the hand, from *manus* hand — more at manual

Date: 12th century

1 a : kind, sort <what manner of man is he>
  b : kinds, sorts <all manner of problems>

2 a (1) : a characteristic or customary mode of acting : custom (2) : a mode of procedure or way of acting : fashion (3) : method of artistic execution or mode of presentation : style
  b plural : social conduct or rules of conduct as shown in the prevalent customs <Victorian manners>
  c : characteristic or distinctive bearing, air, or deportment <his poised gracious manner> d *plural* (1) : habitual conduct or deportment : behavior <mind your manners> (2) : good manners e : a distinguished or stylish air

synonyms see bearing, method

— man·ner·less \-ləs\ *adjective*

"Manners are a mirror in which
One shows his portrait."

– Trenetta Robertson

Action Steps

☐ Sunday ______________________________

____

____

☐ Monday ______________________________

____

____

☐ Tuesday ______________________________

____

____

☐ Wednesday ____________________________

____

____

☐ Thursday _____________________________

____

____

☐ Friday _______________________________

____

____

☐ Saturday _____________________________

____

____

Positive Reinforcement

☐ Sunday

☐ Monday

☐ Tuesday

☐ Wednesday

☐ Thursday

☐ Friday

☐ Saturday

Role Playing

☐ Sunday ____________________

☐ Monday ____________________

☐ Tuesday ____________________

☐ Wednesday ____________________

☐ Thursday ____________________

☐ Friday ____________________

☐ Saturday ____________________

Table-Manners

Growing

☐ Sunday ______________________________

____

____

☐ Monday ______________________________

____

____

☐ Tuesday ______________________________

____

____

☐ Wednesday ______________________________

____

____

☐ Thursday ______________________________

____

____

☐ Friday ______________________________

____

____

☐ Saturday ______________________________

____

____

Notes

May Notes cont.

JUNE

The Positive Word Seed: Listening

lis·ten

Pronunciation: \'li-sən\

Function: *verb*

Inflected Form(s): lis·tened; lis·ten·ing \'lis-niŋ, 'li-sən-iŋ\

Etymology: Middle English listnen, from Old English hlysnan; akin to Sanskrit **śroṣati** he hears, Old English **hlūd** loud

Date: before 12th century

transitive verb archaic : to give ear to :

hearintransitive verb

1 : to pay attention to sound <listen to music>

2 : to hear something with thoughtful attention : give consideration <listen to a plea>

3 : to be alert to catch an expected sound <listen for his step>

— lis·ten·er \'lis-nər, 'li-sən-ər\ *noun*

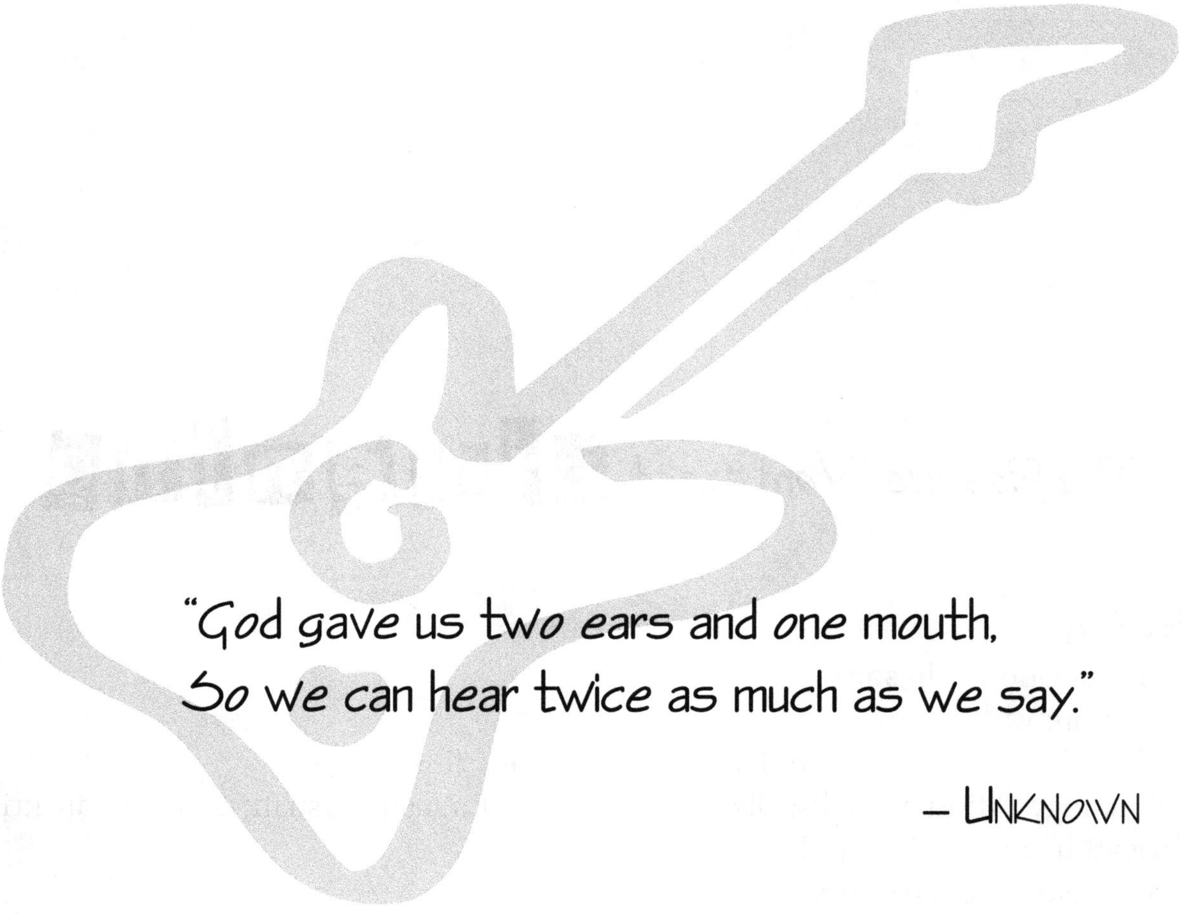

"God gave us two ears and one mouth,
So we can hear twice as much as we say."

– Unknown

Action Steps

☐ Sunday ______________________________

____

____

☐ Monday ______________________________

____

____

☐ Tuesday ______________________________

____

____

☐ Wednesday ____________________________

____

____

☐ Thursday _____________________________

____

____

☐ Friday _______________________________

____

____

☐ Saturday _____________________________

____

____

Positive Reinforcement

☐ Sunday ______________________________

☐ Monday ______________________________

☐ Tuesday ______________________________

☐ Wednesday ______________________________

☐ Thursday ______________________________

☐ Friday ______________________________

☐ Saturday ______________________________

Role Playing

☐ Sunday

☐ Monday

☐ Tuesday

☐ Wednesday

☐ Thursday

☐ Friday

☐ Saturday

June

Listening

Week 4

Growing

☐ Sunday ______________________________

____

____

☐ Monday ______________________________

____

____

☐ Tuesday ______________________________

____

____

☐ Wednesday ______________________________

____

____

☐ Thursday ______________________________

____

____

☐ Friday ______________________________

____

____

☐ Saturday ______________________________

____

____

Notes

June Notes cont.

JULY

The Positive Word Seed: Read

read
Pronunciation: \'**rēd**\
Function: *verb*
Inflected Form(s): **read** \'**red**\; read·ing \'**rē-diŋ**\
Etymology: Middle English **reden** to advise, interpret, read, from Old English **rǣdan**; akin to Old High German **rātan** to advise, Sanskrit **rādhnoti** he achieves, prepares
Date: before 12th century

transitive verb

1 a (1) : to receive or take in the sense of (as letters or symbols) especially by sight or touch (2) : to study the movements of (as lips) with mental formulation of the communication expressed (3) : to utter aloud the printed or written words of <read them a story>
b : to learn from what one has seen or found in writing or printing
c : to deliver aloud by or as if by reading; *specifically* : to utter interpretively
d (1) : to become acquainted with or look over the contents of (as a book) (2) : to make a study of <read law> (3) : to read the works of
e : to check (as copy or proof) for errors f (1) : to receive and understand (a voice message) by radio (2) : To understand.

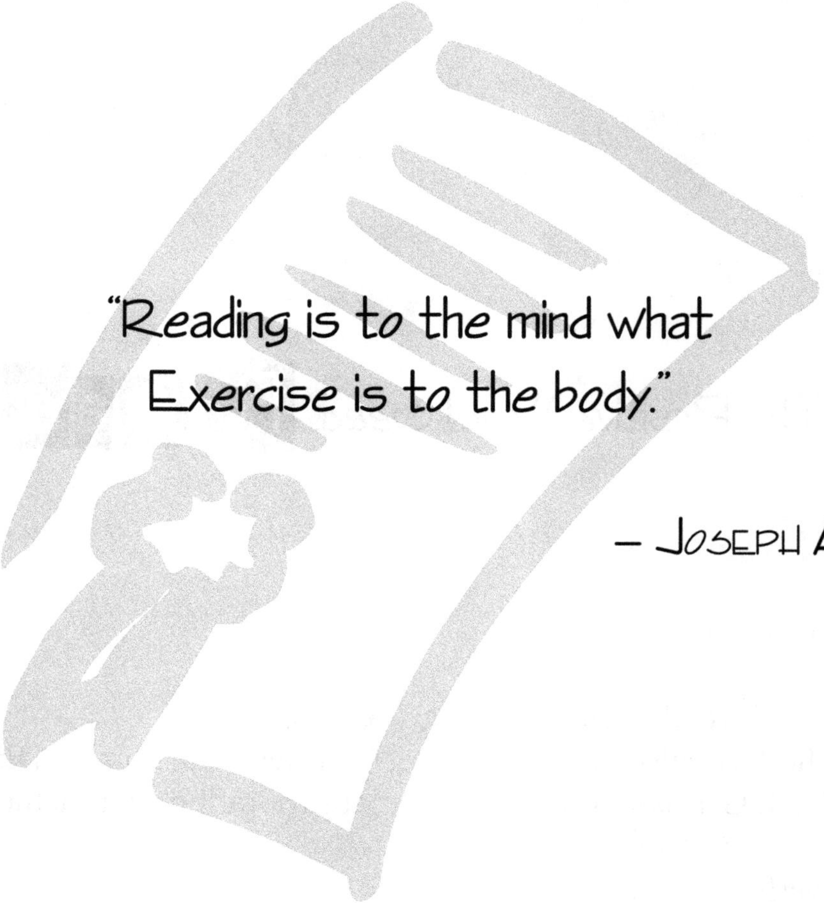

"Reading is to the mind what
Exercise is to the body."

– Joseph Addison

Action Steps

☐ Sunday ______________________________

____

____

☐ Monday ______________________________

____

____

☐ Tuesday ______________________________

____

____

☐ Wednesday ______________________________

____

____

☐ Thursday ______________________________

____

____

☐ Friday ______________________________

____

____

☐ Saturday ______________________________

____

____

Positive Reinforcement

☐ Sunday ______________________________

____

____

☐ Monday ______________________________

____

____

☐ Tuesday ______________________________

____

____

☐ Wednesday ______________________________

____

____

☐ Thursday ______________________________

____

____

☐ Friday ______________________________

____

____

☐ Saturday ______________________________

____

____

Role Playing

☐ Sunday

☐ Monday

☐ Tuesday

☐ Wednesday

☐ Thursday

☐ Friday

☐ Saturday

July

Read

Week 4

Growing

☐ Sunday ______________________________

____

____

☐ Monday ______________________________

____

____

☐ Tuesday ______________________________

____

____

☐ Wednesday ______________________________

____

____

☐ Thursday ______________________________

____

____

☐ Friday ______________________________

____

____

☐ Saturday ______________________________

____

____

Notes

July Notes cont.

AUGUST

The Positive Word Seed: Sharing

share

Function: *verb*

Inflected Form(s): shared; shar·ing

Date: 1590

transitive verb

1 : to divide and distribute in shares : apportion —usually used with *out* <*shared* out the land among his heirs>

2 a : to partake of, use, experience, occupy, or enjoy with others b : to have in common <they share a passion for opera>

3 : to grant or give a share in —often used with with <*shared* the last of her water with us>

4 : to tell (as thoughts, feelings, or experiences) to others —often used with

withintransitive verb

1 : to have a share —used with *in* <we all *shared* in the fruits of our labor>

2 : to apportion and take shares of something

3 : to talk about one's thoughts, feelings, or experiences with others

— shar·er *noun*

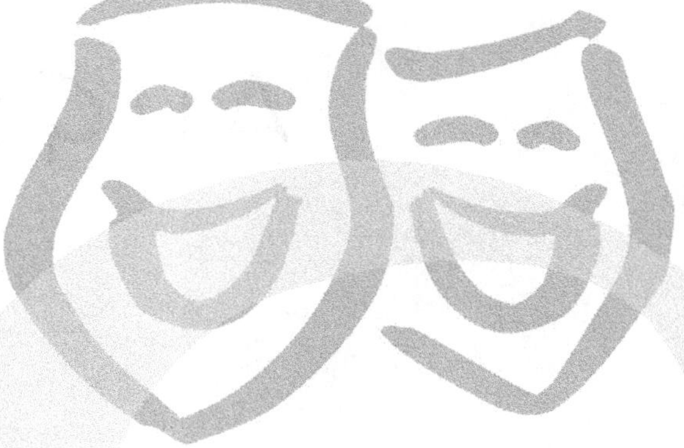

Alone we can do so little.
Together we can do so much.

- Helen Keller

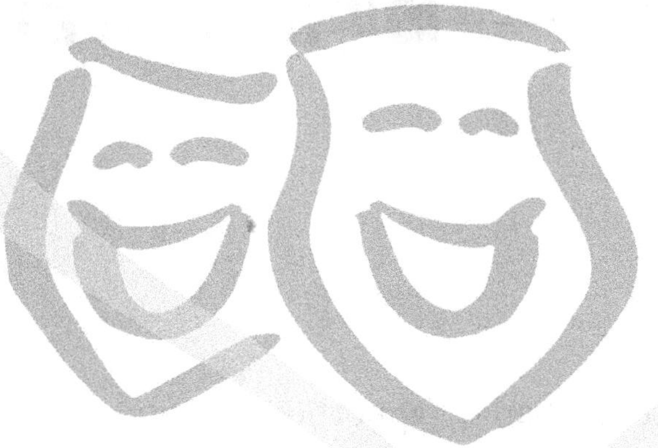

Action Steps

- [ ] Sunday ______________________________

____

____

- [ ] Monday ______________________________

____

____

- [ ] Tuesday ______________________________

____

____

- [ ] Wednesday ______________________________

____

____

- [ ] Thursday ______________________________

____

____

- [ ] Friday ______________________________

____

____

- [ ] Saturday ______________________________

____

____

Positive Reinforcement

☐ Sunday ______________________________

____

____

☐ Monday ______________________________

____

____

☐ Tuesday ______________________________

____

____

☐ Wednesday ______________________________

____

____

☐ Thursday ______________________________

____

____

☐ Friday ______________________________

____

____

☐ Saturday ______________________________

____

____

Role Playing

☐ Sunday ______________________________

____

____

☐ Monday ______________________________

____

____

☐ Tuesday ______________________________

____

____

☐ Wednesday ______________________________

____

____

☐ Thursday ______________________________

____

____

☐ Friday ______________________________

____

____

☐ Saturday ______________________________

____

____

August

sharing week 4

Growing

☐ Sunday ____________________

☐ Monday ____________________

☐ Tuesday ____________________

☐ Wednesday ____________________

☐ Thursday ____________________

☐ Friday ____________________

☐ Saturday ____________________

Notes

August Notes cont.

SEPTEMBER

The Positive Word Seed: Respect

re·spect
Pronunciation: \ri-ˈspekt\
Function: *noun*
Etymology: Middle English, from Latin *respectus*, literally, act of looking back, from *respicere* to look back, regard, from *re-* + *specere* to look — more at spy
Date: 14th century

1 : a relation or reference to a particular thing or situation <remarks having respect to an earlier plan>
2 : an act of giving particular attention : consideration
3 a : high or special regard : esteem
   b : the quality or state of being esteemed
   c *plural* : expressions of respect or deference <paid our respects>

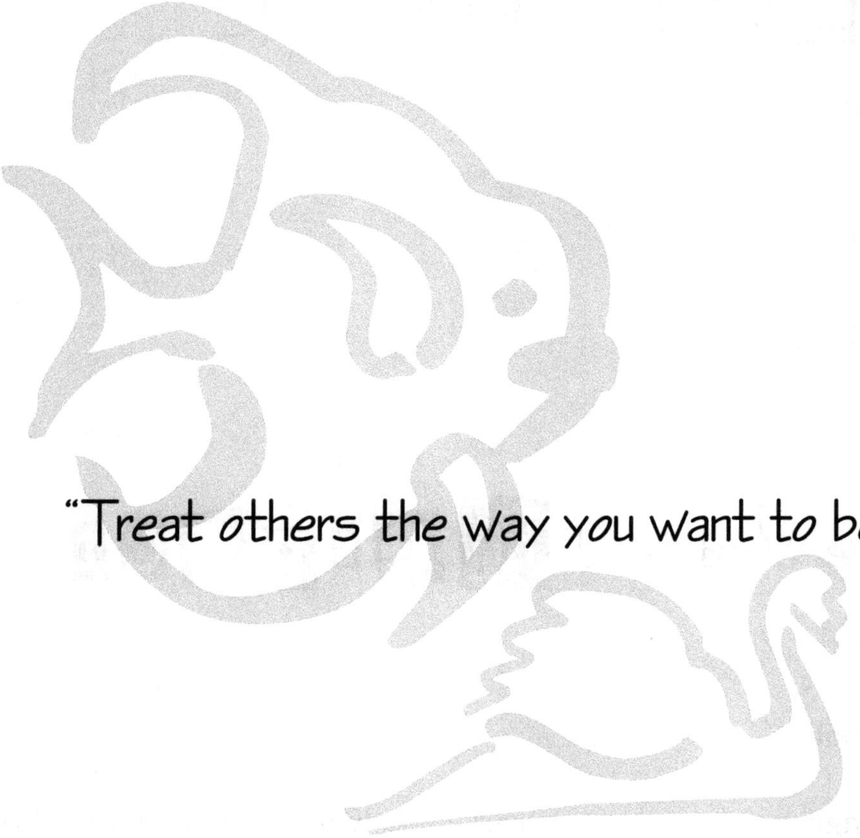

"Treat others the way you want to be treated."

- Holy Bible

Action Steps

☐ Sunday ______________________________

☐ Monday ______________________________

☐ Tuesday ______________________________

☐ Wednesday ______________________________

☐ Thursday ______________________________

☐ Friday ______________________________

☐ Saturday ______________________________

Positive Reinforcement

☐ Sunday ______________________________

____

____

☐ Monday ______________________________

____

____

☐ Tuesday ______________________________

____

____

☐ Wednesday ______________________________

____

____

☐ Thursday ______________________________

____

____

☐ Friday ______________________________

____

____

☐ Saturday ______________________________

____

____

Role Playing

☐ Sunday

☐ Monday

☐ Tuesday

☐ Wednesday

☐ Thursday

☐ Friday

☐ Saturday

Growing

☐ Sunday ______________________________

☐ Monday ______________________________

☐ Tuesday ______________________________

☐ Wednesday ______________________________

☐ Thursday ______________________________

☐ Friday ______________________________

☐ Saturday ______________________________

Notes

September Notes cont.

OCTOBER

The Positive Word Seed: Think

think
Pronunciation: \'thiŋk\
Function: *verb*
Inflected Form(s): thought \'thȯt\; think·ing
Etymology: Middle English *thenken*, from Old English *thencan*; akin to Old High German *denken* to think, Latin **tongēre** to know — more at thanks
Date: before 12th century

transitive verb

1 : to form or have in the mind
2 : to have as an intention <*thought* to return early>
3 a : to have as an opinion <think it's so> b : to regard as : consider <think the rule unfair>
4 a : to reflect on : ponder <think the matter over> b : to determine by reflecting <think what to do next>
5 : to call to mind : remember <he never thinks to ask how we do>
6 : to devise by thinking —usually used with up <*thought* up a plan to escape>
7 : to have as an expectation : anticipate <we didn't think we'd have any trouble>
8 a : to center one's thoughts on <talks and thinks business> b : to form a mental picture of
9 : to subject to the processes of logical thought <think things out>

"Change your thoughts,
And you can change your world."

– Norman Vincent Peale

Think

Action Steps

☐ Sunday ______________________________

____

____

☐ Monday ______________________________

____

____

☐ Tuesday ______________________________

____

____

☐ Wednesday ______________________________

____

____

☐ Thursday ______________________________

____

____

☐ Friday ______________________________

____

____

☐ Saturday ______________________________

____

____

Positive Reinforcement

☐ Sunday ______________________________

____

____

☐ Monday ______________________________

____

____

☐ Tuesday ______________________________

____

____

☐ Wednesday ______________________________

____

____

☐ Thursday ______________________________

____

____

☐ Friday ______________________________

____

____

☐ Saturday ______________________________

____

____

Role Playing

☐ Sunday ______________________________

____

____

☐ Monday ______________________________

____

____

☐ Tuesday ______________________________

____

____

☐ Wednesday ______________________________

____

____

☐ Thursday ______________________________

____

____

☐ Friday ______________________________

____

____

☐ Saturday ______________________________

____

____

October

Think

Week 4

Growing

☐ Sunday ______________________________

☐ Monday ______________________________

☐ Tuesday ______________________________

☐ Wednesday ______________________________

☐ Thursday ______________________________

☐ Friday ______________________________

☐ Saturday ______________________________

Notes

October Notes cont.

NOVEMBER

The Positive Word Seed: Thankful

thank·ful
Pronunciation: \ˈthaŋk-fəl\
Function: *adjective*
Date: before 12th century

1 : conscious of benefit received <for what we are about to receive make us truly thankful>
2 : expressive of thanks <thankful service>
3 : well pleased : glad <was thankful that it didn't rain>
— thank·ful·ness *noun*

"In all things give thanks."

- Holy Bible

Action Steps

☐ Sunday ____________________

☐ Monday ____________________

☐ Tuesday ____________________

☐ Wednesday ____________________

☐ Thursday ____________________

☐ Friday ____________________

☐ Saturday ____________________

Positive Reinforcement

☐ Sunday ____

____

____

☐ Monday ____

____

____

☐ Tuesday ____

____

____

☐ Wednesday ____

____

____

☐ Thursday ____

____

____

☐ Friday ____

____

____

☐ Saturday ____

____

____

Role Playing

☐ Sunday ____________________

☐ Monday ____________________

☐ Tuesday ____________________

☐ Wednesday ____________________

☐ Thursday ____________________

☐ Friday ____________________

☐ Saturday ____________________

Growing

☐ Sunday ______________________________

____

____

☐ Monday ______________________________

____

____

☐ Tuesday ______________________________

____

____

☐ Wednesday ______________________________

____

____

☐ Thursday ______________________________

____

____

☐ Friday ______________________________

____

____

☐ Saturday ______________________________

____

____

DECEMBER

The Positive Word Seed: Growth

growth
Pronunciation: \'grōth\
Function: *noun*
Date: 1557

1 a (1) : a stage in the process of growing : size (2) : full growth
  b : the process of growing
  c : progressive development : evolution
  d : increase, expansion <the growth of the oil industry>
2 a : something that grows or has grown
  b : an abnormal proliferation of tissue (as a tumor)
  c : outgrowth d : the result of growth : product
3 : a producing especially by growing <fruits of his own growth>
4 : anticipated progressive growth especially in capital value and income <some investors prefer growth to immediate income>

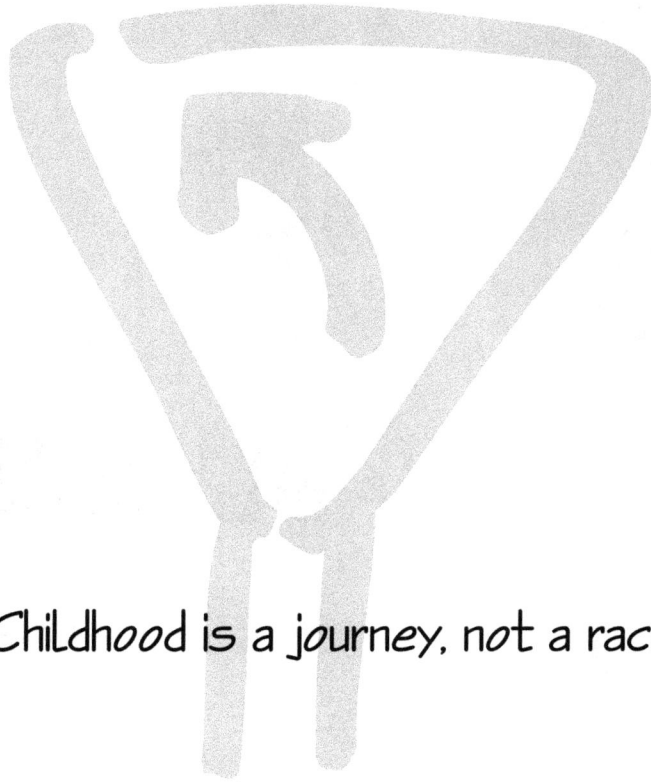

“Childhood is a journey, not a race.

– Unknown

Action Steps

☐ Sunday ______________________________

____

____

☐ Monday ______________________________

____

____

☐ Tuesday ______________________________

____

____

☐ Wednesday ______________________________

____

____

☐ Thursday ______________________________

____

____

☐ Friday ______________________________

____

____

☐ Saturday ______________________________

____

____

Positive Reinforcement

☐ Sunday ______________________________

____

____

☐ Monday ______________________________

____

____

☐ Tuesday ______________________________

____

____

☐ Wednesday ______________________________

____

____

☐ Thursday ______________________________

____

____

☐ Friday ______________________________

____

____

☐ Saturday ______________________________

____

____

Growth

Role Playing

☐ Sunday

☐ Monday

☐ Tuesday

☐ Wednesday

☐ Thursday

☐ Friday

☐ Saturday

Growing

☐ Sunday ______

☐ Monday ______

☐ Tuesday ______

☐ Wednesday ______

☐ Thursday ______

☐ Friday ______

☐ Saturday ______

Notes

December Notes cont.

To order additional copies of

Ms. Sally's

Healthy Habit

CALENDAR JOURNAL

For Kids

have your credit card ready and call
From USA: 1 800-917-BOOK (2665)
From Canada: (877) 855-6732

or e-mail
orders@selahbooks.com

or order online at
www.selahbooks.com

www.ingramcontent.com/pod-product-compliance
Lightning Source LLC
Chambersburg PA
CBHW081339090426
42737CB00017B/3211
* 9 7 8 1 5 8 9 3 0 2 5 1 8 *